GONE TO THE PARK

Gone to the Park, part of the 'Words Together' series, has been created to support children to understand and use two-word sentences.

Using the pivot word 'gone', the simple story and repetitious structure provide an opportunity for the child to hear and experience the sentence structure in new ways. Bright and colourful illustrations provide rich opportunities for conversation and engagement.

This storybook is an exciting resource for early years practitioners, parents, and those working with children at an early stage of speech and language development.

Kate Freeman is a highly experienced speech and language therapist, consultant and former charity director. She is also a mum to three grown-up sons, and a grandmother. Kate's passion is working with children and families, making a difference to their futures.

Kate's career has included working with children, families, groups, local authorities, charities and commercial organisations, providing an insight into the skills of communication and how children learn to talk.

Jenny Edge is a professional artist and illustrator working in a wide range of mediums and styles. She enjoys producing colourful, decorative and ornamental paintings as well as the figurative work she trained in at art school. Although based in Warwickshire, her work can be found all over the world in both domestic and commercial interiors.

GONE TO THE PARK

A 'WORDS TOGETHER' STORYBOOK TO HELP CHILDREN FIND THEIR VOICES

Kate Freeman
Illustrated by Jenny Edge

Routledge
Taylor & Francis Group

LONDON AND NEW YORK

Cover image: © Jenny Edge
First published 2022
by Routledge
2 Park Square, Milton Park, Abingdon, Oxon OX14 4RN

and by Routledge
605 Third Avenue, New York, NY 10158

Routledge is an imprint of the Taylor & Francis Group, an informa business

British Library Cataloguing-in-Publication Data
A catalogue record for this book is available from the British Library

Library of Congress Cataloging-in-Publication Data
Names: Freeman, Kate (Speech therapist), author. | Edge, Jenny, illustrator.
Title: Gone to the park : a Words Together storybook to help children find their voices / Kate Freeman ; illustrated by Jenny Edge.
Description: New York : Routledge, 2022. | Series: Words together |
Summary: Illustrations and simple, repetitive text chronicle a toddler's trip to the park.
Identifiers: LCCN 2021032324 (print) | LCCN 2021032325 (ebook) | ISBN 9781032151823 (pbk) | ISBN 9781003242901 (ebk)
Subjects: CYAC: Toddlers—Fiction. | Parks—Fiction. | LCGFT: Picture books.
Classification: LCC PZ7.1.F75458 Go 2022 (print) | LCC PZ7.1.F75458 (ebook) | DDC [E]—dc23
LC record available at https://lccn.loc.gov/2021032324
LC ebook record available at https://lccn.loc.gov/2021032325

ISBN: 978-1-032–15182-3 (pbk)
ISBN: 978-1-003–24290-1 (ebk)

DOI: 10.4324/9781003242901

Typeset in Candy Randy
by codeMantra

Dedicated to Bryony, Arthur, Chay, Harvey and Sandy, alongside all the children I have cared for and worked with. These people, their families and early years settings are the inspiration for the Words Together series of books.

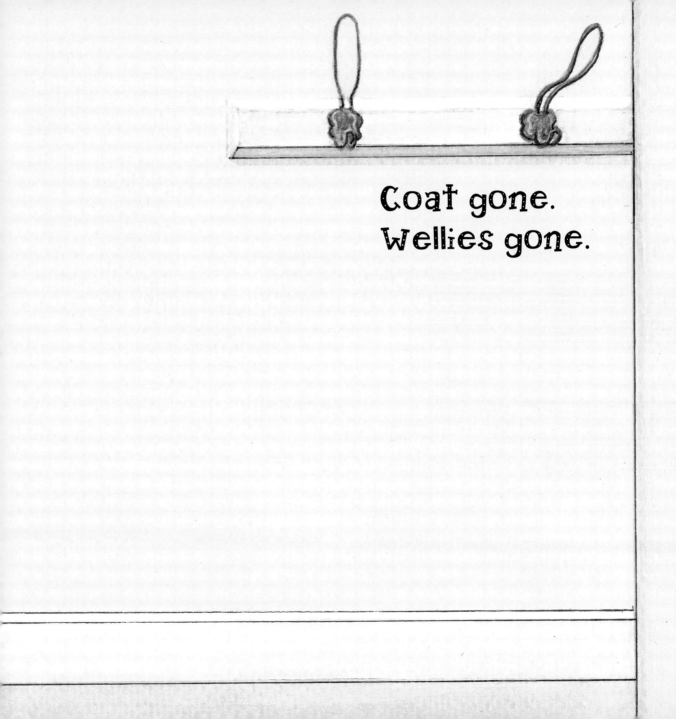

Coat gone.
Wellies gone.

Bee gone

Butterfly gone.

Ladybird
gone.

Food gone.

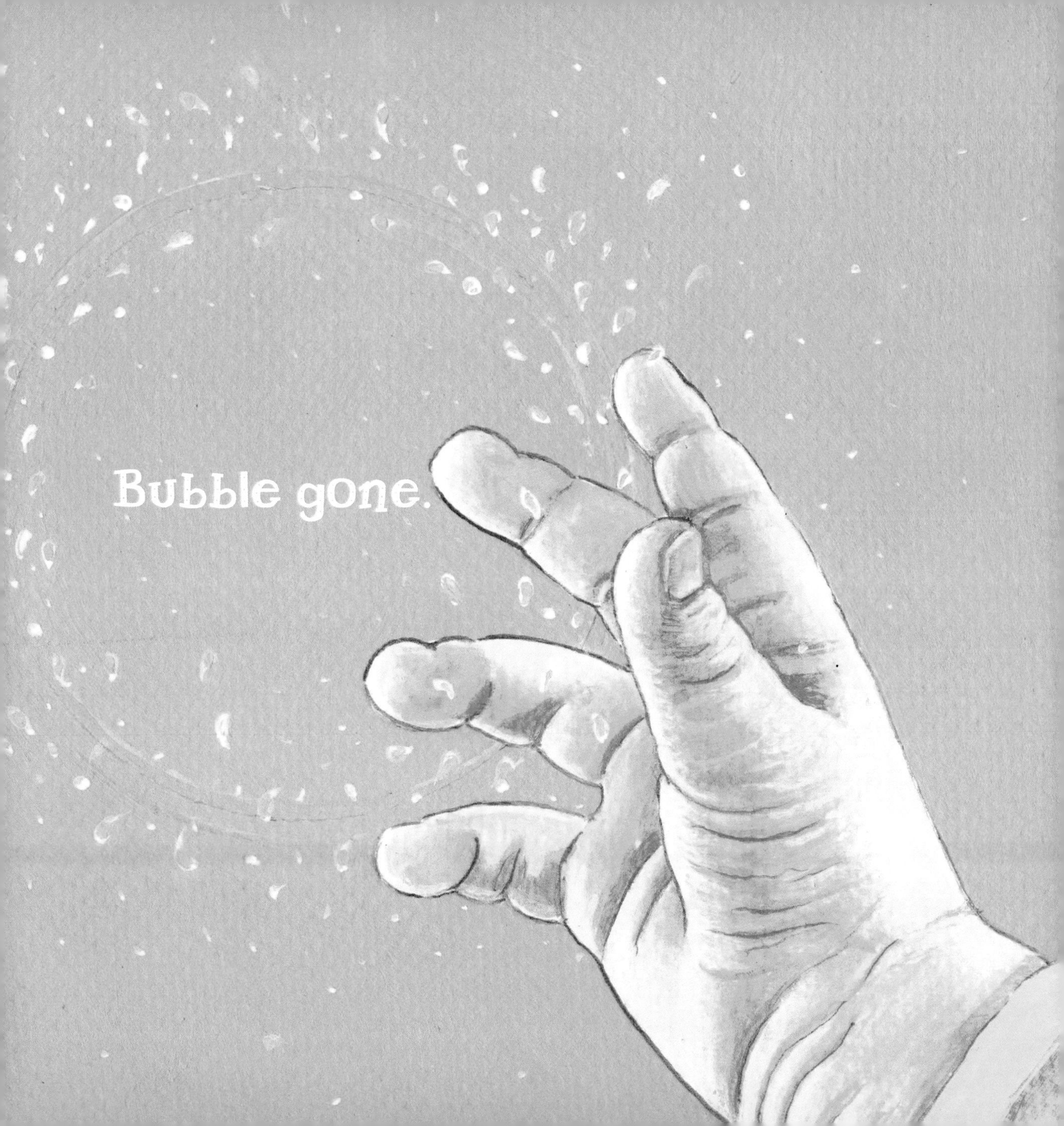

Bubble gone.

Sun gone.

Rain gone.

Clouds gone.

Home time.